Yellow Umbrella Books are published by Red Brick Learning
7825 Telegraph Road, Bloomington, Minnesota 55438
http://www.redbricklearning.com

Library of Congress Cataloging-in-Publication Data
Trumbauer, Lisa
    What is an insect/by Lisa Trumbauer = ¿Qué es un insecto?/por Lisa Traumbauer.
    p. cm.
    Summary: "Simple text and photos present common insects"—Provided by publisher.
    Includes indexes.
    ISBN-13: 978-0-7368-6011-6 (hardcover)
    ISBN-10: 0-7368-6011-8 (hardcover)
    1. Insects—Juvenile literature. I. Title: ¿Qué es un insecto?. II. Title.
QL467.2.T78 2006
595.7—dc22   2005025841

Written by Lisa Trumbauer
Developed by Raindrop Publishing

Editorial Director: Mary Lindeen
Editor: Jennifer VanVoorst
Photo Researcher: Wanda Winch
Adapted Translations: Gloria Ramos
Spanish Language Consultants: Jesús Cervantes, Anita Constantino
Conversion Assistants: Jenny Marks, Laura Manthe

Photo Credits
Cover: Paul Hartley/Image Ideas, Inc.; Title Page: Don W. Abrams; Page 4:
Scott Bauer/USDA/ARS; Page 6: Digital Vision; Page 8: Paul Hartley/Image
Ideas, Inc.; Page 10: Paul Hartley/Image Ideas, Inc.; Page 12: Ruth Adams/Index
Stock; Page 14: Paul Hartley/Image Ideas, Inc.; Page 16: J. M. Burnley/Bruce
Coleman, Inc.

1 2 3 4 5 6 11 10 09 08 07 06

What Is an Insect?

by Lisa Trumbauer

¿Qué es un insecto?

por Lisa Trumbauer

Yellow Umbrella Books
for early readers

4

An ant is an insect.

Una hormiga es un insecto.

A bee is an insect.

Una abeja es un insecto.

A butterfly is an insect.

Una mariposa es un insecto.

A dragonfly is an insect.

Una libélula es un insecto.

A ladybug is an insect.

Una mariquita es un insecto.

A grasshopper is
an insect.

Un saltamontes es
un insecto.

A firefly is
an insect, too!

Una luciérnaga es
un insecto también.

Index

Índice